A Free Gift

I want to say Thank You for buying my book so I put together a free gift for you!

"The Coffee Cocktails Recipe Book"

This gift is the perfect complement to this book so if you want me to send you the free gift head to:

www.GoodLivingPublishing.com/cocktails

Contents

Introduction 7
Your Bar 9
Tools of the Trade 12
Bar Terminology 14
Some Tips to Remember 18
The Recipes 20
The Classic Cocktails 21
    Cosmopolitan 22
    Vieux Carre 23
    Sidecar 24
    Martini 25
    Old Cuban 26
    Negroni 27
    Daiquiri 28
    Old Fashioned 29
    Cuba Libre 30
    Manhattan 31
    Mai Tai 32
    Rob Roy 33
    Margarita 34
    French 75 35
    Dark and Stormy 36
    Mojito 37
    Tom Collins 38
    Sex on the Beach 39
    Rye and Dry 40

- Bloody Mary 41
- Strawberry Daiquiri 42
- Black Russian 43
- Pina Colada 44
- Long Island Ice Tea 45
- Woo-Woo 46
- White Russian 47
- Dry Martini 48
- Gin Sling 49
- French Martini 50
- Kir Royale 51
- Vespa 52
- Strawberry Shortcake 53

The Contemporary Cocktails 54
- Widow Kiss 55
- Ti'Punch 56
- 8 Ward 57
- Picasso Pisco Punch 58
- Pisco Sour 59
- Boulevardier 60
- Twentieth Century 61
- Zombie 62
- Rattlesnake 63
- Jack Rose 64
- Martinez 65
- Singapore Sling 66
- Scofflaw 67
- Japanese 68

Toronto	69
Hemingway	70
Corn n Oil	71
Brown Derby	72
Bijou	73
Blinker	74
Bobby Burns	75
Last Word	76
Ramos Gin Fizz	77
Sazerac	78
Corpse Reviver	79
Aviation	80
Algonquin	81
Air Mail	82
Earl Grey Martini	83
Moscow Mule	84
Twelve Mile Limit	85
Vancouver	86
Diamond Back	87
Caipirinha	88
Humble Pie	89
Agro Dolce	90
Something Dutch	91
Double Truffle Martini	93
Pink Pantie Dropper	94
Bloated Monkey	95
Big Bad Voodoo Kooler	96
Hop Skip and Go Naked	97

Half-Man 98

Donkey Kick 99

A Russian Italian 100

Spartan 101

Apple Pie in the Sky 102

Bees Knees 103

Kinky Kick 104

Plata Fizz 105

Pumpkin Martini 106

Strongbow Spice 107

Liquid Coke 108

Tequila Sunrise 109

Martinez 110

Mint Julep 111

Flaming Asshole 112

Hot Butter Rum 113

Surfer on Acid 114

Blackberry Punch Mixer 115

Boston Cooler 117

Cafe Cabana 118

Citrus Smack 119

Detroit Daisy 120

Sunset Island 121

Alabama Slammer 122

Muay Thai 123

Chicago Punch 124

Enjoy this book? 125

Introduction

Originally the term cocktail was used to refer to a drink that was a mixture of two or more of the following ingredients: spirits, sugar, water and a form of bitters. However in recent times the meaning of the word has expanded and become more colloquial.

These days any type of drink, alcoholic or not, that has a variety of different ingredients is often referred to as a cocktail. That said it is expected that when using the term cocktail, alcohol is going to be involved – and in this book that is certainly the case.

In this beginners guide to making cocktails we will be understanding the term cocktail in the modern sense – an alcoholic drink that is made up of two or more ingredients.

I want to be clear that the purpose of this book is not to teach you how to become a highly trained and skilled mixologist. Getting to this level takes years of dedicated practice and I'm guessing that isn't what you are looking for.

Instead the purpose of the book is to give you delicious cocktail recipes that have all been simplified so that anyone can make them. Whip up these drinks to impress your friends and shock them with your newly acquired and seemingly difficult skill.

In the research for this book I interviewed 24 skilled mixologists and bartenders. I asked them to take their favourite cocktails and strip them down to the simplest form possible. I also asked them to list their essential tools and tips for beginners so that anyone can whip up awesome cocktails with apparent ease.

As you read through this book you are going to learn the following:

- How to make over 100 cocktails

- How to make your own home bar

- The essential equipment you need to make amazing cocktails

- The terminology and secret language of bartenders

- Tips and tricks for making sure your cocktails always turn out amazing

Work through the book and in no time at all you will be able to whip up amazing drinks wherever you go.

So, get ready to impress your friends whilst enjoying some amazing cocktails.

Your Bar

One of the most important aspects of making high quality, delicious cocktails in your home is having a bar. A bar that is well-stocked, has the necessary tools and that you are familiar with will improve the cocktails you make drastically.

Knowing your bar and having the necessary ingredients means that you won't run into problems such as ice melting in your drink, liquor sitting in fruit too long as well as a host of other issues. Although what I just said may seem trivial these small changes will ruin cocktails quicker than anything else.

The term bar doesn't just refer to the typical bars you see in clubs, pubs and…bars – instead it can be viewed as any area that is used to mix and serve drinks.

If you were thinking that owning your own bar is something for only wealthy then read through this section and see just how easily and cheaply you can create your own full-service home bar.

Having a bar in your house is very easy to set up and need not cost a lot of money. I like to always tell people that they have three different options when it comes to building a home bar. These will be discussed now and then you can pick the right one for you. Please note, that each of these bars also requires certain cocktail making tools (not to mention alcohol), which will be discussed later.

The Mobile Bar

The mobile bar is quick, easy and very low cost. Due to its mobility it is good for entertaining but the size of it can be limiting – I prefer to keep the mobile bar for one-on-one gatherings. I will have decided what drinks to serve ahead of time and set the bar accordingly.

To have your own mobile bar you will need only an aesthetically appealing tray. The tray acts as both the serving and the preparation surface. As the mobile bar will only be used for the actually mixing and serving of the drinks (not the storage of ingredients) you will need to store your ingredients elsewhere. When it comes time to make cocktails just add what you need to the tray and carry out to where you are going to be mixing.

The Half and Half

This is what I recommend for most people as it brilliantly blends functionality and aesthetics with ease of storage and cost.

A half and half is the middle ground between a mobile bar and a full bar. The best example, and what I suggest you use, is a trolley - ideally one which will have two or three levels.

The lower level, or tray, is used to store bottles (you can easily store 15+ bottles on one of these) and the upper is for your tools, equipment and mixing. A half and half takes up more space than a mobile bar but you free up storage elsewhere as your equipment and liquors are stored on the trolley. Plus if you have an eye for design you can make it a feature of the room that is rolled out for parties.

A Half and Half is absolutely brilliant if you are having a party or entertaining - just wheel it and have people request their favourite cocktails.

The Full Bar

A full bar is awesome.

However it takes up space, costs a lot to install and will most likely become the central attraction of your house. If that doesn't bother you though then a full bar is the pinnacle.

A full bar is a scaled down version of everything you would get in a regular bar/club and has a fridge, a sink and taps, glass storage, liquor shelves and a seating area.

Tools of the Trade

Now you know the 3 styles of home bars it is time to stock your bar with the necessary equipment.

As this is a beginner's book I won't go overboard on the equipment, instead I've stripped this section down to the bare minimum. All the cocktails in this book can be made with the following equipment and each piece listed can be picked up at a price to suit any budget.

Cocktail Shaker

Either comes as one piece that has a tightly fitting cap with a strainer built into the cap or comes as two pieces – a mixing glass with a metal bar-tin. The latter is what you see in movies and is referred to as a Boston shaker.

Mixing Glass

A glass you will use when stirring drinks to mix. If you choose to buy a shaker that doesn't come with a mixing glass then you can use a high-ball glass instead.

Strainer

A strainer is used after mixing and whilst pouring. The purpose of it is to pour the shaken or stirred drink from your shaker into your glass without fruit or ice.

Jigger

Measuring devices that are conical in shape and hold set amounts – usually 1 & ½ oz., ¾ oz. and 1 oz.

Bar Spoon

Different from an ordinary spoon due to its length and thinness. Used to stir drinks.

Muddler

Used to crush and mix ingredients together.

Ice Bucket

The name says it all. Buying an ice bucket means you won't have to run to the freezer every time you need more ice. As many cocktails requires a great deal of ice this will save you a lot of hassle.

Glasses

Throughout the cocktail recipes in this book you will notice I mention several different types of glasses. I suggest you buy at least 4 of each of these to avoid running out – again these can all be picked up for any budget. Check your local dollar store, often you will find gorgeous glasses for $1.

- Highball Glass. A tall, thin glass for serving long cocktails or mixed drinks.

- Rocks Glass. A short, stumpy glass with a wide base. Often referred to as a whiskey glass.

- Shot Glass/Shooter. A very small glass that can usually only contain 2oz. of liquid. If you don't own jiggers then you can also use these for rough measurements.

- Martini/Cocktail Glass. The classic cocktail glass that is synonymous with cocktails and you will have seen a million times.

Bar Terminology

I wanted to include this terminology section for a few reasons.

Firstly, as you work through the recipes in this book you will see several of the terms being used. I tried to limit the use of bartending and mixologist terminology but using some has to be expected.

Secondly, I want this book to not only teach you how to make cocktails but also be an introduction to the whole world of mixology and cocktails. I want you to be able to go into a bar, have a conversation with a bartender and impress him/her with your knowledge.

No more being confused when they throw confusing words at you. No more having to ask your waitress what a "Shrub" is and wondering why it's been used in your drink.

Although you don't need to learn these terms, study them or to be honest with you even read this section – I wanted to include it to give you as much value as possible and make this book your complete guide.

The Terms

Aperitif

A drink served prior to eating. The purpose of this is to stimulate one's appetite in preparation for a meal.

Box

To mix ingredients of the drink quickly without shaking them. Shaker will be turned once and then poured into a glass.

Call Drink

A drink that has a brand which is used in the name and emphasised over the other ingredients. A simple example would be a Sailors and Coke – Sailor Jerry mixed with coke and fresh lime.

Cobbler

Any drink that is served in a high-ball glass with crushed ice, mint leaves and fruit.

Chaser

A drink, usually non-alcoholic, that is drank straight after a shot. This is used for two purposes – either to null the taste of the shot or to emphasis a certain flavour within the shot.

Digestif

A drink served post eating. The purpose is to aid digestion. Examples would be Sambuca, Port or an espresso laced with liqueur.

Lace

The last ingredient added to a cocktail recipe. Often added after the cocktail has been mixed and added to the glass.

Fizz

Does not refer to champagne or Prosecco, instead it simple means any drink that is carbonated. You may hear a bartender or mixologist "adding fizz" which could simply mean soda water.

Frappe

A partially frozen beverage.

High-Ball

Any spirit served with soda/sparkling water in a tall glass, which is where the term high-ball glass comes from.

Low-Ball

Any spirit served with soda/sparkling water in a short glass. Short glass refers to a rocks-glass.

Mist

A drink, usually an after dinner liqueur, poured into a short glass of crushed ice. Name comes from the mist that will rise as the alcohol touches the ice.

Neat

A drink served without ice or any accompanying ingredients. Drink is poured straight from bottle into the serving glass.

Nip

An amount equal to ¼ of a bottle.

Nightcap

A pre-sleep drink.

On the Rocks

A drink served over cubes of ice.

Pick Me Up

A particular type of drink designed for the morning after drinking. These can be either alcoholic or non-alcoholic. The most famous example would be a Bloody Mary or a Virgin Mary.

Shrub

A combination of spirits, fruit/juice from a fruit and sugar aged in an air-tight container.

Straight Up

A drink that is shaken or stirred with ice but then strained into serving glass with the ice excluded.

Sour

A cocktail or shot that contains a spirit, sugar and lemon or lime juice.

Tot

A small measure

Virgin

Drink containing no alcohol. A Virgin Mary is the most famous example.

With a Twist

A twist is piece of lemon or lime peel (and sometimes orange) that has been peeled from the fruit and placed in the drink. If peeled properly a twist will twist itself into shape, however this requires some skill and it is often easier to peel and then manually twist over a straw before adding.

Some Tips to Remember

Again this book has been designed so that all the cocktails are delicious whilst very hard to screw up.

The most common way that beginners mess up cocktail mixing is by forgetting a few key tips.

These tips are simple and might seem trivial but they can make all the difference between an okay drink and an awesome one.

- Always chill your glasses, unless stated otherwise. Do this by placing a few ice cubes in the glass and ideally a splash of water. Before pouring the cocktail drain the glass and give a gentle shake. You can also place glasses in fridge for an hour before serving.

- Always have plenty of ice available.

- Need crushed ice? Wrap tightly in a kitchen/bar towel and break against a surface or using your muddler.

- Whenever possible use freshly squeezed fruit juice.

- Before juicing fruit be sure to roll it with your hand applying moderate pressure. Doing this before cutting the fruit will result in much more juice being released when you go to squeeze.

- Don't fill the shaker to the brim with ice. Leave room for the ingredients to move.

- Always hold glasses by the bases and the stems, nothing ruins the appearance of a cocktail like finger marks.

- A good indication of a well shaken drink is when the outside of the shaker begins to frost.

- Do not let ice rest too long in the shaker/mixing glass. The ice will begin to melt and dilute the alcohol.

- When creating twists or using peel be sure to exclude the membrane of the peel. Use only the skin.

- If your fruit slices, wedges and chunks are looking past their best cover them in soda water and place in the fridge to revitalize.

- When shaking, unless stated otherwise, use a short range of motion and shake at a high speed. Use two hands.

- Ensure your cutting knife is very sharp and always cut away from your body. This is of incredible importance when cutting peels or twists.

- When rimming the glass with sugar ensure the edge is damp. Having a damp edge will cause the sugar to stick to the rim.

The Recipes

In this part of the book you will often see the ingredient "syrup" mentioned – this is simply a sugar and water mix that is used in cocktails. To make it follow these instructions below.

To make syrup combine equal parts very hot water and sugar to a mixing cup. Muddle this and allow to sit for 3 hours. Pour into a bottle to store if making in advance. Ideally you want to make the syrup on the day you will be serving cocktails but I understand this isn't always possible – so store in the fridge if making in advance. If the syrup comes out too thick add warm water and mix.

Now, let's go make some cocktails.

The Classic Cocktails

Cosmopolitan

Ingredients

1 & ½ oz. vodka

1 oz. cranberry juice

½ oz. triple sec

½ oz. freshly squeezed lime juice

Directions

Add all ingredients to a shaker filled with ice.

Shake well and strain into a cocktail glass.

Serve with a garnish of a lime wedge.

Vieux Carre

Ingredients

1 oz. rye

1 oz. cognac

1 oz. Vermouth

1/4 oz. Benedictine

Dash of Peychaud's bitters

Dash of angostura bitters

Direction

Add ingredients to a shaker filled with ice.

Shake well and serve in a rock-glass over crushed ice.

Garnish with a lemon twist.

Sidecar

Ingredients

2 oz. brandy

1 oz. triple sec

½ oz. freshly squeezed lemon juice

Pinch of brown sugar

Directions

Add ingredients, except the sugar, to a shaker filled with ice.

Shake well and strain into a rocks-glass.

Rim the glass with sugar and serve.

Martini

Ingredients

2 & ½ oz. gin

½ oz. vermouth

Dash of orange bitters

Directions

Add all ingredients to a high-ball glass filled with ice.

Stir well and strain.

Garnish with a lemon twist.

Old Cuban

Ingredients

1 & ½ oz. dark rum

1 oz. syrup

¾ oz. freshly squeezed lime

6 mint leaves, torn

3 dashes angostura bitters

Directions

Muddle the mint and add to a shaker.

Add the other ingredients and ice to the shaker.

Shake well and strain.

Top off with generous splash of champagne.

Negroni

Ingredients

1 oz. gin

1 oz. vermouth

1 oz. Campari

Directions

Add ice to a rocks-glass and add ingredients.

Stir well and garnish with an orange twist.

Daiquiri

Ingredients

2 oz. white rum

1 oz. freshly squeezed lime

1 oz. syrup

Directions

Add all ingredients to a shaker filled with ice.

Shake well and strain.

Garnish the drink with a lime wheel.

Old Fashioned

Ingredients

2 oz. bourbon

2 sugar cubes

1 dash of angostura bitters

Directions

Muddle the sugar with the bitters until well crushed.

Add to a high-ball glass with the bourbon and stir well.

Strain over a rocks-glass.

Garnish with a twist of orange.

Cuba Libre

Ingredients

2 oz. rum

½ oz. lime

4 oz. coke

Directions

Add the rum and lime to a shaker filled with ice.

Shake well and then strain over a rocks-glass with crushed ice.

Add the coke and garnish with a lime wedge.

Manhattan

Ingredients

2 oz. rye

1 oz. vermouth

2 dashes angostura bitters

Directions

Add ingredients to a shaker cup and shake well.

Pour into a cocktail glass and garnish with a twist of orange or a cherry.

Mai Tai

Ingredients

2 oz. blend of light and dark rum

1 oz. lime

¾ oz. Orgeat syrup

½ oz. triple sec

Directions

Add crushed ice to a rocks-glass and build drink over the ice.

Garnish with mint and serve.

Rob Roy

Ingredients

2 oz. scotch

1 oz. vermouth

1 dash of angostura bitters

Directions

In a rocks-glass add ice cubes.

Pour ingredients in and stir well.

Garnish with a cherry.

Margarita

Ingredients

1 & ½ oz. tequila

1 oz. cointreau

½ oz. lime

Pinch of sea salt

Directions

Add ingredients, minus the salt, to a high-ball glass with ice and stir well.

Strain into a rocks-glass filled with ice.

Rim glass with salt.

French 75

Ingredients

4 oz. Champagne

1 oz. gin

1 teaspoon of sugar

¼ oz. freshly squeezed lemon juice

Directions

Add the sugar and lemon juice to a champagne flute and muddle gently.

Pour in the gin and muddle again.

Add the champagne and stir gently.

Dark and Stormy

Ingredients

Ginger Beer

2 oz. dark rum

2 lime wedges

Directions

Add the ginger beer to a high-ball glass filled with ice.

Squeeze one lime wedge into the ginger beer and then discard.

With a teaspoon slowly and carefully add the rum. You want the rum to sit on the top of the ginger beer so do not pour too quickly.

Mojito

Ingredients

2 oz. rum

1 oz. freshly squeezed lime juice

4 oz. lemonade/sparkling water/soda water

7 mint leaves

2 teaspoons brown sugar

Directions

Add the lime, sugar and 6 mint leaves to a shaker and muddle.

Ideally you want to let this rest for several hours, however you don't need to if time doesn't allow.

Fill a high-ball glass with ice, add the muddled lime mix to the glass.

Pour in the rum and stir.

Top off with sparkling drink and garnish with 1 mint leaf.

Tom Collins

Ingredients

2 oz. gin

¾ oz. freshly squeezed lemon juice

¾ oz. syrup

5 oz. soda water

Directions

Add the gin, lemon juice and syrup to a cocktail shaker filled with ice.

Fill a high-ball glass with ice and soda water.

Strain the gin mixture into the soda water and garnish with a lime wheel.

Sex on the Beach

Ingredients

1 & ½ oz. vodka

¾ oz. peach schnapps

½ oz. creme de cassis

2 oz. orange juice

2 oz. cranberry juice

Directions

Pour everything into a shaker filled with ice cubes.

Shake well and then strain into a high-ball glass filled with ice.

Garnish with a cherry and twist of orange.

Rye and Dry

Ingredients

2 oz. Canadian Club

6 oz. dry ginger ale

Directions

Pour into a high-ball glass with ice.

Bloody Mary

Ingredients

1 oz. of vodka

Tomato juice

1 teaspoon Tabasco sauce

2 dashes of Worcestershire sauce

½ oz. of freshly squeezed lemon juice

Salt

Pepper

Stalk of celery

Directions

Pour tomato juice into a glass filled with ice. Do not fill to the top though, leave around 2 cm to rim.

Add the vodka, Tabasco, Worcestershire and lemon juice. Stir well.

Sprinkle in a dash of salt and pepper then add the celery stick and use this to stir the drink. You can then add a lemon wheel for garnish but this is optional.

Strawberry Daiquiri

Ingredients

1 oz. white rum

½ oz. Crème de fraises

½ oz. freshly squeezed lemon juice

4 Strawberries

½ cup of crushed ice

Directions

Add all the ingredients to a blender and pulse for 15 seconds.

Pour into a chilled glass and garnish with a strawberry.

Black Russian

Ingredients

2 oz. vodka

1 oz. Kahlua

Coke

Directions

Add the vodka and Kahlua to a shaker and shake well.

Pour into a rocks-glass of ice and top off with coke.

Pina Colada

Ingredients

2 oz. golden rum

½ oz. Cream of coconut

1 teaspoon cream

3 oz. pineapple juice

1 Orange wedge

Directions

Add ingredients to a blender and pulse for 20 seconds.

Pour into a high-ball filled with ice.

Long Island Ice Tea

Ingredients

½ oz. gin

½ oz. white rum

½ oz. tequila

1 oz. vodka

½ oz. triple sec

Coke

Freshly squeezed lime juice

Freshly squeezed lemon juice

1 Lemon wedge

½ teaspoon syrup

Directions

Add all the ingredients, except the coke, to a shaker filled with ice and shake well.

Strain into a high-ball glass half filled with crushed ice.

Top off with coke.

Woo-Woo

Ingredients

1 & ½ oz. peach schnapps

1 oz. vodka

Cranberry juice

Directions

Add all ingredients to a high-ball glass filled with ice and stir.

White Russian

Ingredients

2 oz. vodka

1 oz. Kahlua

Cream

Directions

Shake the vodka and Kahlua together before pouring into a rocks-glass filled with ice.

Float cream over this.

Dry Martini

Ingredients

3 oz. gin

½ oz. Martini Bianco

1-2 green olives

Directions

Add the gin and vermouth to a high-ball glass filled with ice and stir well for 15 seconds.

Strain into a chilled cocktail glass.

Stick the olives onto a cocktail stick and add.

Gin Sling

Ingredients

3 oz. gin

1 oz. cherry brandy

Soda water

½ oz. Lemon juice

4 Maraschino cherry

Directions

Add the brandy, gin, lemon juice to a shaker filled with ice and shake well.

Layer crushed ices and cherries in a high-ball glass and top off with soda water.

French Martini

Ingredients

2 oz. vodka

¼ oz. raspberry flavoured liqueur

1 oz. pineapple juice.

Directions

Add all ingredients to a shaker filled with ice.

Shake well and strain into a chilled cocktail glass.

Kir Royale

Ingredients

Champagne

1 oz. Crème de cassis

Directions

Pour champagne into a flute and top off with crème de cassis

Vespa

Ingredients

2 oz. gin

1 oz. vodka

2 oz. dry white wine

Directions

In a highball glass add the ingredients and stir slowly for 30 seconds.

Pour into a chilled cocktail glass and add a twist of lemon and one of lime.

Strawberry Shortcake

Ingredients

2 oz. Amaretto

1 oz. Cream

Handful of strawberries

½ cup of ice

Directions

Add ingredients to a blender and pulse for 30 seconds.

Pour this into a chilled wine glass.

Sugar the rim and serve

The Contemporary Cocktails

Widow Kiss

Ingredients

1 & ½ oz. apple brandy

¾ oz. Benedictine

¾ oz. yellow Chartreuse

2 dashes of angostura bitters

Twist of lemon

Directions

Add all ingredients to a tall glass or shaker, filled with ice.

Stir well and then strain into a high-ball glass.

Ti'Punch

Ingredients

2 oz. Rhum Agricole

¼ oz. squeezed lime juice from a lime wedge

¼ oz of cane sugar

Directions

Add the sugar into a rocks glass and squeeze in the lime juice.

Drop the wedge into the glass and stir well.

Pour in the rum and stir well.

Serve over crushed ice.

8 Ward

Ingredients

2 oz. rye whiskey

½ oz. freshly squeezed lemon juice

½ oz. freshly squeezed orange juice

1 tsp grenadine

1 Cherry, Maraschino is best

Directions

Add all ingredients, except the cherry to a shaker.

Add a handful of ice and shake well.

Strain into a rocks-glass and garnish with cherry

Picasso Pisco Punch

Ingredients

2 oz. Pisco

¾ oz. fresh lemon and lime juice mix

½ oz. pineapple juice

Distilled water, small splash

Directions

Add all ingredients to shaker filled with ice.

Shake well and strain into high-ball glass.

Garnish with a pineapple wedge

Pisco Sour

Ingredients

3 oz. Pisco

1 oz. syrup

1 oz. freshly squeezed lime juice

1 egg white

Directions

Add all ingredients to a shaker (ice is optional, I prefer dry)

Shake well and pour into rocks-glass

Drip angostura bitters in as garnish

Boulevardier

Ingredients

1 & ½ oz. Bourbon

1 oz. Campari

1 oz. Vermouth

Directions

Add all ingredients to a shaker filled with ice.

Stir well and strain into a cocktail glass.

Garnish with an orange twist

Twentieth Century

Ingredients

1 & ½ oz. gin

¾ oz. Lillet

¾ oz. Creme de Cacao

¾ oz. freshly squeezed lemon juice

Directions

Add all ingredients to a high-ball glass filled with ice.

Stir well and pour into a rocks-glass. Can be served with or without the ice.

Serve with a lemon twist for garnish

Zombie

Ingredients

2 oz. rum, you can use multiple rums if you want to create a blend.

1 oz. 151 proof Demerara rum

2 oz. freshly squeezed lemon & lime mixturee

1 oz. pineapple juice

1 oz. passion fruit syrup

1 teaspoon of brown sugar

1 dash angostura bitters

Directions

Add all ingredients to a shaker filled with ice.

Shake well and strain into a rocks-glass.

Rim the glass with lime and add more bitters to taste

Rattlesnake

Ingredients

2 oz. rye

¾ oz. freshly squeezed lemon juice

½ oz. maple syrup

1 egg white

1 dash of absinthe

Directions

Combine all ingredients in a glass and stir well.

Jack Rose

Ingredients

1 & ½ oz. Applejack

½ oz. freshly squeezed lime juice

½ oz. grenadine

Directions

Add all ingredients to a shaker filled with ice.

Shake well and serve

Martinez

Ingredients

1 & ½ oz. gin

1 & ½ oz. Vermouth

Dash of Maraschino liquor

Angostura bitters, one or two dashes

Dash of orange bitters

Directions

Add all ingredients to a high-ball glass and stir well.

Transfer to a rocks-glass and serve

Singapore Sling

Ingredients

1 & ½ oz. gin

½ oz. Cherry Heering

¼ oz. Benedictine

¼ oz. triple sec

½ oz. lime

1 & ½ oz. pineapple juice

3 dashes angostura bitters

Directions

Add ingredients to a shaker filled with ice and shake well.

Pour into high-ball glass and top off with soda water.

Garnish with one cherry and a lime wheel.

Scofflaw

Ingredients

1 & ½ oz. rye

1 oz. Vermouth

¾ oz. freshly squeezed lemon juice

¾ oz. grenadine

2 dashes of orange bitters

Directions

Add all ingredients to shaker filled with ice.

Shake well and strain into high-ball glass

Japanese

Ingredients

2 oz. cognac

½ oz. Orgeat syrup

1 dash angostura bitters

Directions

In a high-ball glass filled with ice add all the ingredients.

Gently stir and then serve with a twist of lemon

Toronto

Ingredients

2 oz. Canadian whisky

¼ Fernet Branca

¼ syrup

2 dashes of angostura bitters

Directions

Add to a shaker filled with ice and stir well.

Strain into cocktail glass.

Flame a slice of orange peel and squirt over drink.

Use flamed peel as garnish

Hemingway

Ingredients

2 oz. white rum

½ oz. grapefruit juice

¾ oz. freshly squeezed lime juice

¼ oz. syrup

¼ oz. Maraschino liqueur

Directions

Add all ingredients to a shaker filled with ice.

Shake well and strain.

Corn n Oil

Ingredients

2 oz. dark rum

½ oz. Falernum syrup

1 dash of angostura bitters

Directions

In a rocks-glass add crushed ice.

Build the cocktail over the ice.

Garnish with a lime wedge

Brown Derby

Ingredients

2 oz. bourbon

1 oz. grapefruit

½ oz. honey syrup

Directions

Add ingredients to a shaker filled with ice and shake well.

Strain over a cocktail glass

Bijou

Ingredients

1 oz. gin

1 oz. green chartreuse

1 oz. vermouth

Dash of orange bitters

Directions

Add ingredients to a rocks-glass with or without ice.

Stir gently and garnish with a cherry

Blinker

Ingredients

2 oz. rye

1 oz. grapefruit juice

½ oz. raspberry syrup

Directions

Add to a shaker and shake well.

Pour into a rocks-glass and garnish with a twist of lemon.

Bobby Burns

Ingredients

1 & ½ oz. scotch

1 & ½ oz. vermouth

1 teaspoon Benedictine

Directions

Add ice to a rocks-glass and build the drink over the top.

Stir once or twice and garnish with a twist of lemon.

Last Word

Ingredients

¾ oz. gin

¾ oz. freshly squeezed lime juice

¾ oz. green Chartreuse

¾ oz. Maraschino liqueur

Directions

Add ingredients to a shaker and shake well.

Strain into a cocktail glass and serve

Ramos Gin Fizz

Ingredients

2 oz. gin

1 oz. whipping cream

1 egg white

½ oz. lemon juice

½ oz. lime juice

1 oz. syrup

2-3 drops orange flower water

1 dash of vanilla extract

Directions

Add ingredients to shaker and shake well.

Add ice and then shake again for 30 seconds.

Strain into a high-ball glass and top off with soda water.

Sazerac

Ingredients

1 teaspoon syrup

3 dashes Peychaud's bitters

2 oz. rye whiskey

Dash of absinthe

Lemon wedge

Directions

Add ingredients, except lemon, to a high-ball glass filled with ice and stir well.

Strain into a rocks-glass and squeeze lemon over the cocktail

Corpse Reviver

Ingredients

¾ oz. gin

¾ oz. Lillet

¾ oz. triple sec

¾ oz. freshly squeezed lemon juice

Dash of absinthe

Directions

Add ingredients to a shaker filled with ice.

Shake well and strain into a glass.

Serve with ice or without

Aviation

Ingredients

1 & ½ oz. gin

½ oz. freshly squeezed lemon juice

½ oz. Maraschino liquor

¼ oz. Liqueur de Violette

Directions

Add ingredients to a rocks-glass and stir well.

Add crushed ice and garnish with a cherry.

Algonquin

Ingredients

1 & ½ oz. rye

¾ oz. vermouth

¾ oz. pineapple juice

Directions

Add ingredients to a shaker filled with ice.

Shake well and strain over a cocktail glass.

Garnish with a wedge of pineapple.

Air Mail

Ingredients

1 oz. rum

½ oz. freshly squeezed lime juice

½ oz. honey syrup

Sparkling wine.

Directions

Add the ingredients, except the wine, to a shaker filled with ice and shake.

Pour into a champagne flute and top off with sparkling wine.

Garnish with angostura bitters and a mint leaf.

Earl Grey Martini

Ingredients

2 oz. gin

1 Earl Grey Teabag

½ oz. lemon juice

¼ oz. syrup

Directions

Place the earl grey tea bag in the gin and leave for several hours.

Add the infused gin, lemon juice and syrup to a shaker filled with ice. Shake well and strain into a cocktail glass.

Rim the edge with brown sugar.

Moscow Mule

Ingredients

1 & ½ oz. vodka

3 oz. ginger beer

1 lime.

Directions

Add vodka and ginger beer to a rocks-glass filled with ice.

Stir well and squeeze half a lime over the drink.

Drop the lime half into the drink and serve.

Twelve Mile Limit

Ingredients

1 oz. white rum

½ oz. rye whiskey

½ oz. brandy

½ oz. grenadine

½ oz. freshly squeezed lemon juice

Directions

Add all ingredients to a shaker filled with ice.

Shake well and strain over a cocktail glass.

Garnish with a twist of lemon.

Vancouver

Ingredients

2 oz. gin

½ oz. sweet vermouth

1 teaspoon Benedictine

2 dashes of orange bitters

Directions

Add all ingredients to a high-ball glass filled with ice.

Stir well for around 20-30 seconds.

Strain into a cocktail glass and add a lemon twist as garnish

Diamond Back

Ingredients

1 & ½ oz. rye whiskey

¾ oz. Applejack

¾ oz. green Chartreuse

Directions

Add all ingredients to a high-ball glass filled with ice.

Stir well for around 20-30 seconds.

Strain into a cocktail glass and add a cherry as garnish

Caipirinha

Ingredients

2 teaspoons sugar

2 limes, quartered into wedges

2 oz. Cachaça

Directions

Add the limes to a shaker and sprinkle the sugar over the top. Muddle this together.

Add crushed ice to the shaker and pour in the Cachaca.

Shake well and pour into a rocks-glass.

Humble Pie

Ingredients

1 oz. orange infused vodka

1 oz. Aperol

¼ oz. freshly squeezed lemon juice

Club soda

Directions

Add the vodka, Aperol and lemon juice to a shaker filled with ice.

Shake well and strain into a high-ball glass filled with crushed ice.

Top off with Soda water and garnish with two lemon wheels

Agro Dolce

Ingredients

1 & ½ oz. of lemon infused vodka

½ oz. balsamic syrup (see below for instructions)

½ a lemon

For the balsamic syrup:

Rind from one orange

½ cup white balsamic

½ cup sugar

1 cup water

To make the balsamic syrup
Add the ingredients to a pot and bring to the boil. Let simmer stirring frequently.
Reduce until mixture becomes a thick syrup.

Directions

Rim the martini glass with lemon and sugar.

Add the vodka and syrup to a shaker filled with ice and shake well.

Strain into the rimmed martini glass and serve with a twist of lemon.

Something Dutch

Ingredients

1 & ½ oz. Bols Genever

1 oz. Pineau Des Charentes Rosé

¾ oz. rhubarb and strawberry mix (see below for instructions)

½ oz. lemon juice

½ oz. syrup

1 dash of orange bitters

To make the rhubarb mix:

1 lb diced rhubarb

1 pint strawberries

1 tablespoon dried Angelica root

Juice and zest of 1 lemon

1 cup Champagne vinegar

1 cup white sugar

To make rhubarb mix:
Add all the ingredients (except the vinegar and sugar) to a pot and bring to the boil. Let simmer until the rhubarb breaks down.

Pass through a cloth or very fine sieve into a bowl. Add the vinegar and sugar and stir well.

Store in a bottle once mixture has cooled.

Directions

Add all ingredients to a shaker with two ice cubes.

Shake well and strain into a cocktail glass.

For garnish drip a few drops of freshly squeezed lemon juice into the drink.

Double Truffle Martini

Ingredients

3 oz. vodka

½ oz. dry vermouth

½ oz truffle juice

1 Truffle-stuffed olive

Directions

Add ingredients, excluding the olive, to a shaker filled with ice.

Shake well and strain into a martini glass.

Garnish with the truffle olive

Pink Pantie Dropper

Ingredients

1 & ½ oz. of gin

1 oz. tequila

1 Scoop vanilla ice cream

4 oz. pink lemonade

Directions

Add gin, tequila and ice cream to a blender and pulse.

Pour into a high-ball glass and top off with pink lemonade

Bloated Monkey

Ingredients

1 oz. white rum

1 oz. peach schnapps

½ oz. Grand Marnier

1 oz. pineapple juice

1 oz. orange juice

1 Maraschino cherry

Directions

Add all ingredients to a high-ball glass filled with ice.

Stir well and strain into a cocktail glass.

Add the cherry for garnish.

Big Bad Voodoo Kooler

Ingredients

2 oz. Malibu

1 oz. dark rum

1 oz. Midori

2 oz. orange juice

2 oz. pineapple juice

Soda water

Directions

Add the Malibu, the rum and the Midori to a high-ball glass with 3 ice cubes.

Stir well before topping off the fruit juices. Stir again.

Add a splash of soda-water to top off the drink.

Hop Skip and Go Naked

Ingredients

¼ oz. cherry brandy

¼ oz. vodka

¼ oz. triple sec

½ oz. freshly squeezed lime juice

Orange juice, enough to top off the drink

½ oz. grenadine.

Directions

Add everything except the orange juice and grenadine to a shaker filled with ice.

Shake well and strain into a high-ball glass.

Top off with orange juice and stir once.

Once drink has stopped moving carefully float the grenadine on top.

Half-Man

Ingredients

1 & ½ oz. white rum

½ oz. peach schnapps

¼ oz. Scotch

2 oz, passion fruit juice

2 oz. orange juice

¼ oz. grenadine

Directions

Add the ingredients to a cocktail glass in the order listed above.

Stir once and then let the drink settle.

Carefully float the grenadine on top.

Donkey Kick

Ingredients

½ oz. gin

½ oz. brandy

1 oz. Benedictine

½ oz. apricot brandy

½ oz. maple syrup

Directions

Add ingredients to a shaker filled with ice.

Flip once to blend ingredients then strain into a cocktail glass.

A Russian Italian

Ingredients

1 oz. Amaretto

1 oz. Malibu

1 oz. vodka

1 oz. cranberry juice

1 oz. pineapple juice

Directions

Add all ingredients to a shaker filled with ice.

Shake well and strain into a cocktail glass.

Spartan

Ingredients

½ oz. Jagermeister

1 oz. spiced rum

½ oz. gold tequila

6 oz. tomato juice

1 teaspoon tabasco sauce

Directions

Add all ingredients to a shaker.

Shake well and pour over crushed ice in a high-ball glass.

Apple Pie in the Sky

Ingredients

Champagne

2 oz. apple juice

¼ oz. liquid honey

½ oz. cinnamon schnapps

Directions

Add all the cinnamon, honey and apple juice to a champagne flute and gently stir.

Top off with champagne, or Prosecco

Bees Knees

Ingredients

1 & ¼ oz. dry gin

¾ oz. freshly squeezed lemon juice

¾ oz. honey

Champagne

Directions

Add the gin, lemon juice and honey to a shaker filled with ice.

Shake well and strain into a champagne flute.

Top off with champagne

Garnish with a raspberry

Kinky Kick

Ingredients

1 & ½ oz. vodka

1 oz. freshly squeezed lime juice

1 oz. syrup

3 cherries

Champagne

Directions

Add the cherries to the shaker and muddle them.

Pour the vodka, lime and syrup into the shaker and add small amount of crushed ice.

Shake well and strain into a glass filled with ice-cubes.

Top off with champagne and garnish with mint.

Plata Fizz

Ingredients

1 oz. Silver Patrón

1 oz. Elderflower liqueur

Peeled orange slice

Champagne

Directions

Add the orange peel to a shaker and muddle.

Add the patron, elderflower to the shaker and top off with ice.

Shake well and strain into a champagne flute.

Top off with champagne and garnish with a twist of orange.

Pumpkin Martini

Ingredients

2 oz. vodka

2 oz. pumpkin spiced liqueur

2 teaspoons of whipped cream

1 small piece of cinnamon stick

Directions

Add the vodka and liqueur to a rocks-glass with 5 ice cubes.

Stir well and top with the whipped cream.

Garnish with a cinnamon stick.

Strongbow Spice

Ingredients

4 oz. Strongbow cider

1 & ½ oz. cinnamon infused whiskey

1 oz. pomegranate juice

1 teaspoon pomegranate seeds

Directions

Pour the cider into a high-ball glass filled with ice.

Add the whiskey and pomegranate juice and gently stir.

Drop in the teaspoon of pomegranate seeds.

Liquid Coke

Ingredients (do not drink more than one of these)

1 oz. Bacardi 151

1 oz. Goldschläger

1 oz. Rumple Minze

1 oz. Jägermeister

Directions

Add all ingredients to rocks-glass filled with ice.

Stir gently once.

Tequila Sunrise

Ingredients

2 oz. of tequila

½ oz. of Grenadine

Orange Juice

Directions

Add the orange to a high-ball glass filled with ice.

Pour in the tequila and stir once.

Float the grenadine and serve with an orange wheel.

Martinez

Ingredients

1 & ½ oz. of gin

1 & ½ oz. sweet vermouth

½ oz. maraschino liqueur

2 dashes of orange bitters

Directions

Add the ingredients to a shaker glass half filled with crushed ice.

Stir well and then strain into a rocks-glass.

Garnish with a twist of lemon.

Mint Julep

Ingredients

2 oz. bourbon

2 teaspoons of syrup

7 leaves fresh mint

Mint sprig

Directions

Add the syrup to the bottom of a high-ball glass and drop the mint leaves on top.

Muddle and then fill the glass with filled ice.

Pour in the bourbon and then garnish with mint sprigs.

Flaming Asshole

Ingredients

¼ oz. grenadine syrup

¼ oz. creme de menthe

¼ oz. creme de bananes

¼ oz. white rum

Directions

In a shallow glass layer the grenadine, crème de menthe, crème de bananes and white rum.

Carefully light the drink with a long stemmed lighter or match.

Hot Butter Rum

Ingredients

1 slice butter

1 teaspoon brown sugar

½ teaspoon ground cinnamon

Vanilla extract

1 oz. dark rum

Hot water

Directions

Add the butter, sugar and spices to a mug or thick glass.

Add one teaspoon of hot water and mix well.

Pour in the rum and then top off with hot water, stir well.

Surfer on Acid

Ingredients

1 & ½ oz. of Jagermeister

½ oz. of Malibu

1 oz. of pineapple juice

Directions

Add the pineapple juice to a rocks glass filled with ice.

Pour in the Malibu and stir.

Carefully float the jagermeister and let it sink into the drink.

Blackberry Punch Mixer

Ingredients

1 oz. dark rum

2 oz. blackberry liqueur

1 teaspoon sugar

2 oz. freshly squeezed lemon juice

Directions

Combine all ingredients in a shaker half filled with ice and shake well.

Strain into a cocktail glass and garnish with a twist of lemon.

Banana Sunrise

Ingredients

1 oz. creme de bananes

1 oz. Pina Colada mix

½ oz. Malibu

3 oz. fresh orange juice

Directions

Add all the ingredients to a shaker filled with ice.

Turn over twice to mix the ingredients and then strain into a high-ball glass.

Garnish with an orange wheel.

Boston Cooler

Ingredients

2 oz. white rum

1 oz. freshly squeezed lemon juice

1 teaspoon white sugar

4 oz. soda water

Directions

Add half the soda water, teaspoon and lemon juice to high-ball glass and muddle the sugar.

Add crushed ice and stir well before adding the rum.

Top off with soda water and garnish with two twists of lemon.

Cafe Cabana

Ingredients

2 oz. coffee flavoured liqueur

3 oz. club soda

Directions

Pour the coffee liqueur into the soda water and serve.

Citrus Smack

Ingredients

1 & ½ oz. rum

1 & ½ oz. triple sec

1 oz. sweet and sour mix

Grapefruit juice

2 pieces of orange peel

Directions

Add ice to a high-ball glass and add the rum, triple sec and sour mix.

Stir well before filling the remainder of the glass with grapefruit juice.

Add the orange peel as garnish

Detroit Daisy

Ingredients

2 oz. dark rum

Half of a lime

1 dash white rum

Directions

Add the two rums to a shaker filled with ice.

Squeeze in the half lime and then drop into the shaker.

Shake well for 30 seconds and strain into a shot glass.

Garnish with mint

Sunset Island

Ingredients

1 & ½ oz. pineapple juice

1 oz. grape juice

1 & ½ oz. soda water

Half of a lemon

1 teaspoon syrup

Directions

Squeeze lemon into a shaker filled with ice and then add the other ingredients.

Shake well and strain into a high-ball glass.

Alabama Slammer

Ingredients

1 oz. gin

1 oz. whisky

1 oz. Galliano

1 oz. triple sec

Fresh orange juice

Directions

Add everything, except the orange juice, to a high-ball and stir well.

Add two cherries to the mix and muddle.

Add crushed ice and then top off with orange juice.

Muay Thai

Ingredients

1 oz. dark rum

1 oz. vodka

1 oz. lemon schnapps

1 oz. lemon juice

1 oz. fresh orange juice

2 oz. tea, chilled to room temperature

1 lemon wedge

1 orange wedge

1 oz. syrup

Directions

Combine all ingredients in a shaker and shake for 30 seconds.

Strain into a high-ball glass half filled with crushed ice.

Float any orange juice foam onto the top of the drink

Chicago Punch

Ingredients

½ oz. Southern Comfort

1 oz. vodka

½ oz. Amaretto

2 oz. fresh orange juice

1 oz. pineapple juice

1 dash of lime cordial

1 dash of Grenadine

Directions

Add all ingredients to a shaker filled with ice and shake well.

Strain into a glass filled with ice and garnish with a wheel of lemon and a wheel of lime.

Enjoy this book?

Please leave a review and let others know what you liked about this book?

Reviews are so crucial to self-published authors like myself and it would mean the world to me if you could leave me a quick review.

Even one sentence would make a huge difference to me!

Thanks,

Andy

All rights Reserved. No part of this publication or the information in it may be quoted from or reproduced in any form by means such as printing, scanning, photocopying or otherwise without prior written permission of the copyright holder.

Disclaimer and Terms of Use: Effort has been made to ensure that the information in this book is accurate and complete, however, the author and the publisher do not warrant the accuracy of the information, text and graphics contained within the book due to the rapidly changing nature of science, research, known and unknown facts and internet. The Author and the publisher do not hold any responsibility for errors, omissions or contrary interpretation of the subject matter herein. This book is presented solely for motivational and informational purposes only.

Printed in Great Britain
by Amazon